Children's illustrations are courtesy of students at Bicentennial Elementary and Ledge Street School, both in Nashua, NH, Ossipee Central School in Center Ossipee, NH, Tuftonboro Central School in Center Tuftonboro, NH, and Lin-Wood Public School, in Lincoln, NH.

Seeking the Wolf Tree

WRITTEN BY
Natalie Cleavitt

ILLUSTRATED BY
Marjorie Leggitt

TAYLOR TRADE PUBLISHING
Lanham • Boulder • New York • London

Published by Taylor Trade Publishing
An imprint of The Rowman & Littlefield Publishing
Group, Inc.
4501 Forbes Boulevard, Suite 200, Lanham, Maryland
20706
www.rowman.com

Unit A, Whitacre Mews, 26-34 Stannary Street, London
SE11 4AB

Distributed by NATIONAL BOOK NETWORK

Copyright © 2015 by Natalie Cleavitt

Illustrations copyright © 2015 by Majorie Leggitt and
Natalie Cleavitt

Library of Congress Cataloging-in-Publication Data
Available
ISBN: 978-1-63076-145-5 (cloth)
ISBN: 978-1-63076-146-2 (electronic)

The paper used in this publication meets the
minimum requirements of American National
Standard for Information Sciences—Permanence
of Paper for Printed Library Materials, ANSI/NISO
Z39.48-1992.

Printed in the United States of America

To the spirits of the old trees and all who seek
their company. —NC

To all the wonderful flora and fauna that
provide an endless stream of subjects to
sketch. —ML

Acknowledgments:

This material is based upon work supported by the
National Science Foundation under grant no. DEB
1346857. Preparation of this book was supported
by the National Science Foundation through the
Long-Term Ecological Research at Hubbard Brook
Experimental Forest grants (DEB 9810221, 0423259,
1114804) to Timothy Fahey. The Hubbard Brook
Committee of Scientists, especially Tim Fahey and
Peter Groffman, have shown constant support for this
project since sending me to the first LTER children's
book conference in 2004. Brian Cleavitt, Melody
Wooster, Nick Grant, Tim Fahey, Cindy Wood, John
Battles, Lynn Christenson, and two generous forest
rangers at the Campton Visitor's Center all provided
character models for the book. Reference photos
used for the illustrations were all taken by the author,
except the nestling photograph by Scott Schwenk.
Theresa Howell was the best editor ever: positive,
clever, and even-handed. Amy Rinehart, series editor,
Rick Rinehart of Taylor Trade Publishing, and Diane
McKnight of the editorial committee have been
stalwart supportersof this Schoolyard series. —NC

**Character notebooks and
sidebar illustrations by
author Natalie Cleavitt**

Any opinions, findings,
and conclusions or
recommendations expressed
in this material are those
of the author and do not
necessarily reflect the views
of the National Science
Foundation.

About the Long Term Ecological Research (LTER)
Network (lternet.edu)

The LTER network is a large-scale program supported by the National
Science Foundation. It consists of 25 ecological research projects, each
of which is focused on a different ecosystem. The goals of the LTER
network are:

Understanding: To understand a diverse array of ecosystems at
multiple spatial and temporal scales.

Synthesis: To create general knowledge through long-term
interdisciplinary research, synthesis of information, and development
of theory.

Information: To inform the LTER and broader scientific community by
creating well-designed and -documented databases.

Legacies: To create a legacy of well-designed and -documented
long-term observations, experiments, and archives of samples and
specimens for future generations.

Education: To promote training, teaching, and learning about long-
term ecological research and the Earth's ecosystems, and to educate a
new generation of scientists.

Outreach: To reach out to the broader scientific community, natural
resource managers, policymakers, and the general public by providing
decision support, information, recommendations, and the knowledge
and capability to address complex environmental challenges.

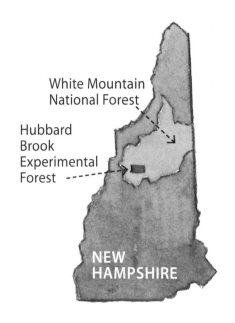

White Mountain National Forest

Hubbard Brook Experimental Forest

NEW HAMPSHIRE

Today is the day Aurora **and** Orion **have** been waiting for—their **first big** field trip to the Hubbard Brook **Experimental** Forest.

We need your help! Grab your notebooks and let's solve the mystery of the wolf tree.

"Come with me!" Orion says, dragging Aurora over to a wall display in the far corner of the visitor's center. "This is what most of the forests in the mountains looked like hundreds of years ago."

"Do you think any of those trees are still alive?" Aurora wonders.

"Maybe. It says right here that 'an **old growth forest** is one in which there has been no large disturbance for at least two hundred years. In these forests, natural **succession** has led to a mixture of trees of all ages and stages, including many unusually old trees.'"

"Wouldn't it be amazing to find a group of old trees like that?" Aurora says.

"Yes, but it sounds like old growth forests are pretty rare these days," Orion comments.

"Still …" Aurora sighs, dreaming of a stand of tall, ancient trees.

"Hey, here's another display about old trees: 'The Wolf Tree.'" Orion laughs and howls like a wolf. He takes out his notebook.

"I've never heard of such a thing!" says Aurora. "It says, 'Old-time foresters coined the term "wolf tree" for trees they saw as having the ability to "eat" the sun and nutrients and prevent the growth of other trees. Today, however, we understand how wolf trees benefit wildlife.

'A wolf tree appears as the largest and oldest tree in the new forest stand. They often have large trunks and low branches from growing in full sunlight. They are impressive because of their size, character, and age, and are commonly surrounded by smaller trees.'"

"That's something we need to find!" Orion exclaims. "Let's go!"

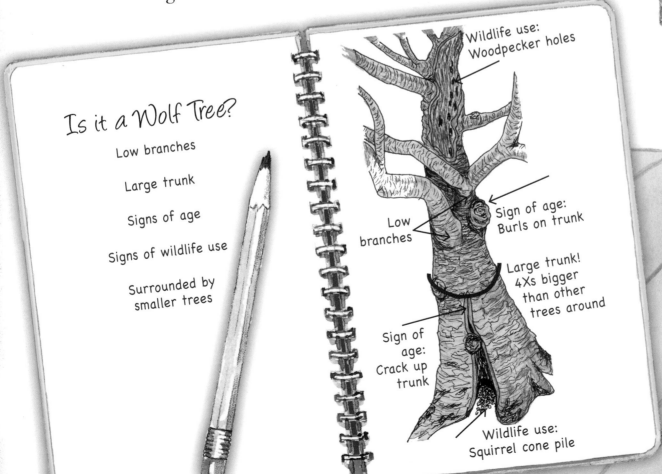

Is it a Wolf Tree?

Low branches

Large trunk

Signs of age

Signs of wildlife use

Surrounded by smaller trees

Wildlife use:
Woodpecker holes

Low branches

Sign of age:
Burls on trunk

Large trunk!
4Xs bigger
than other
trees around

Sign of
age:
Crack up
trunk

Wildlife use:
Squirrel cone pile

"Where should we begin?" Aurora asks, looking at the map.

"Let's begin at one of the **gage stations**," Orion says.

"Hmm, I think we should start in the bird area or maybe in the hemlock ravine," Aurora says.

"How about the **watersheds** or Mount Kineo?" Orion gestures toward the tallest mountain on the map.

"What will we need to bring?" Aurora asks.

HUBBARD BROOK EXPERIMENTAL FOREST

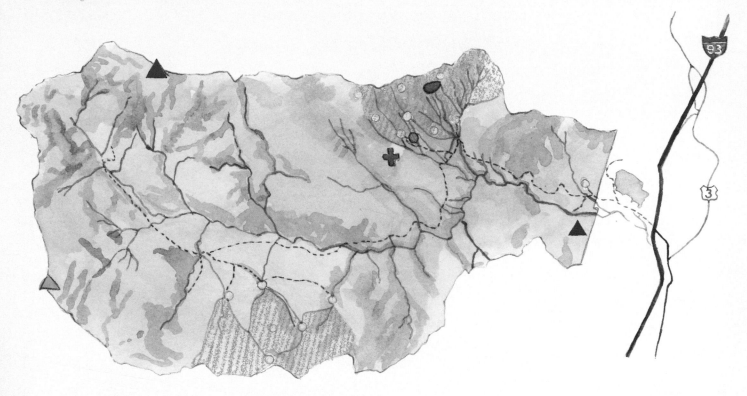

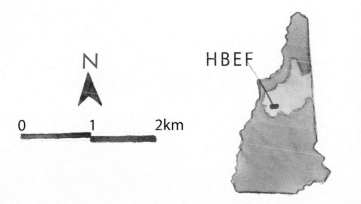

- 🍃 Leaf Collections
- ✚ Bird Area
- ▲ Mt. Cushman
- ● Weir 6
- ▲ Mt. Kineo
- ▲ Hemlock Area
- ○ Gage Stations
- ▨ Watersheds

N

0   1   2km

HBEF

It is MID-SPRING in the forest and the black flies are out! Aurora and Orion have decided to start their quest for a wolf tree in the bird area, where they are going to watch birds and count caterpillars.

"Don't forget your binoculars!" Aurora reminds Orion.

"Do you know if there might be a wolf tree nearby?" Aurora asks Sara, their guide.

Sara knows of a large sugar maple tree she thinks might be one.

"Are wolf trees important to birds?" Orion asks.

"Yes, birds use wolf trees, especially birds called cavity nesters," Sara says. "Before we go look, could you help me identify as many bird nests as possible?"

Oven bird nest

Ruby-throated hummingbird nest

In the afternoon, Orion and Aurora are in the lab helping to count and weigh caterpillars collected from the leaves and saplings in the forest.

Caterpillars are important to the diets of many forest birds. The number and the size of caterpillars differ from year to year, depending on changes in the temperature and rainfall. In years with a cold or wet spring, there are fewer caterpillars and baby birds are hungry.

As they are looking at caterpillars, Orion and Aurora almost forget about the search for the wolf tree. But Sara remembers.

When they return to the forest to release the caterpillars, Sara says, "You guys have been a big help. Thanks! Now let me show you that large sugar maple I was talking about. Let's see if you think it's a wolf tree."

IS THE SUGAR MAPLE A WOLF TREE?

CHECKLIST FOR WOLF TREE

- ☐ Low branches
- ☑ Large trunk
- ☑ Signs of age
- ☑ Signs of wildlife use
- ☐ Surrounded by smaller trees

It is a hot day in **SUMMER**. Aurora and Orion have planned to go to a cool hemlock forest by Hubbard Brook. A professor named Tim needs help collecting soil samples near spots with mushrooms. He is interested in how the tree roots and mushrooms help each other.

"The mushrooms help tree roots gather water and nutrients from the soil, and the roots feed the mushrooms," he explains. "There are lots of mushrooms on the other side, so let's cross the brook. I also know a very large hemlock tree on the other side that I'd like to show you."

Orion and Aurora wonder if it might be a wolf tree.

Scarlet waxy caps
Hygrocybe cantherillis

Black trumpet
Craterellus fallax

Fairy stool
Coltricia cinnamomea

Fly agaric
Amanita muscaria

Coral fungus
Clavulina sp.

Bolete
Boletus affinis

Mushroom hunting is a lot of fun. Aurora and Orion try to imagine how far beneath the soil the mushrooms grow.

"I wonder how many mushrooms are attached to the roots of *this* one? It's so big and old," Orion says, pointing to a very large tree.

"That's the large hemlock!" Tim exclaims.

IS
THE
HEMLOCK
A WOLF
TREE?

CHECKLIST FOR WOLF TREE

- ☐ Low branches
- ☑ Large trunk
- ☐ Signs of age
- ☑ Signs of wildlife use
- ☐ Surrounded by smaller trees

AUTUMN is an exciting time, with changing leaves and animals scurrying to put food away for the winter. On this trip, Aurora and Orion will help Cindy, a forest naturalist, collect leaves and seeds from baskets in the forest. What they collect will tell them a lot about **production**, the number of leaves, and **composition**, the type of leaves.

Hearing of their interest in large trees, Cindy wants to show them her special beech tree high up on the south-facing watersheds.

Yellow birch
Betula allegheniensis

Sugar maple
Acer saccharum

The hike to the top of the watershed is tough. While everyone stops to take a sip of water, Cindy tells them that **mast years** are when the maple and beech trees produce lots of seeds.

"The number of seeds in the forest is important to many animals, including chipmunks and black bears. During mast years, these animals are more likely to survive the winter. More seeds mean more chipmunks in spring. More chipmunks in spring mean trouble for baby birds. Did you know that chipmunks eat baby birds?"

"That's disgusting!" Orion remarks. "I thought they just ate nuts."

As they reach the beech tree at the top of the watershed, they notice black marks in the smooth bark.

"Are those … claw marks?" Aurora asks.

Cindy smiles. "Yes, those are black bear claw marks."

"From the size of them … that was a pretty big bear!" Orion exclaims.

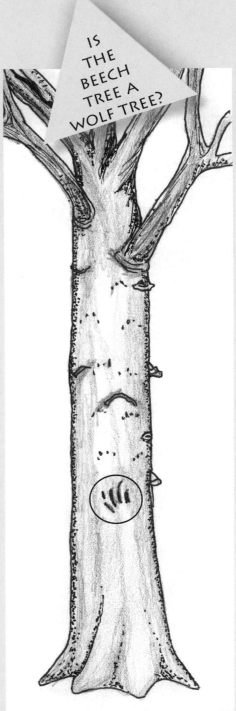

IS
THE
BEECH
TREE A
WOLF TREE?

CHECKLIST FOR WOLF TREE

- ❑ Low branches
- ☑ Large trunk
- ❑ Signs of age
- ☑ Signs of wildlife use
- ☑ Surrounded by smaller trees

It's **MUD SEASON**! Aurora and Orion have waited all winter, wondering if they'll ever find a wolf tree! Nick, a Forest Service hydrologist, takes them in a special vehicle down a very soft, muddy road to visit **gage stations**. They park by a stream with a weir, which measures water flow.

"Every week I come out here to measure temperature, rainfall, and stream water in the forest. The temperature and water affect all the plants and animals in the forest," Nick says. "I am happy to have your help this week."

"Have you ever seen a wolf tree?" Orion asks.

"There's a large yellow birch near one of the highest gage stations," he gestures. "Most of the yellow birches were left by the old-time loggers because they were too crooked to be valuable timber."

Weighing rain gage

Standard rain gage with open bucket

Chart recording rainwater weight

Nick and Orion wrap a special tape measure around the yellow birch tree to find its **diameter**, how wide the tree is. Aurora takes notes.

"This is the fattest tree I've ever seen!" Orion says, trying to reach his arms around for the end of the measuring tape.

"Who do you think lives in here?" Aurora asks, peeking into a cavity at the base of the tree.

"This tree has weathered a few storms," remarks Nick, looking up at the broken canopy.

"This must be our wolf tree!" Aurora and Orion exclaim. "It's got everything: low branches, a large trunk, signs of age and of wildlife use, plus, it's surrounded by much smaller trees."

Howling ensues!

IS THIS BIRCH A WOLF TREE?

CHECKLIST FOR WOLF TREE

- ☑ Low branches
- ☑ Large trunk
- ☑ Signs of age
- ☑ Signs of wildlife use
- ☑ Surrounded by smaller trees

It's SUMMER vacation. During their quest for a wolf tree, Orion and Aurora have come to love the forest and want to return. Today, they accompany Lynn and John, two researchers who study how moose affect forest structure.

"Will we see a moose today?" Orion asks Lynn.

Lynn points out the animal tracks along the way. In the soft mud of the trail, they spot tracks and signs of moose, coyote, a red fox, and mice.

As the four climb, Lynn points to a clump of fir trees that have been nibbled.

"Who would eat sticky fir trees?" Orion asks. "That would be worse than a day-old peanut butter sandwich."

"Firs are the main winter food of the moose," Lynn explains.

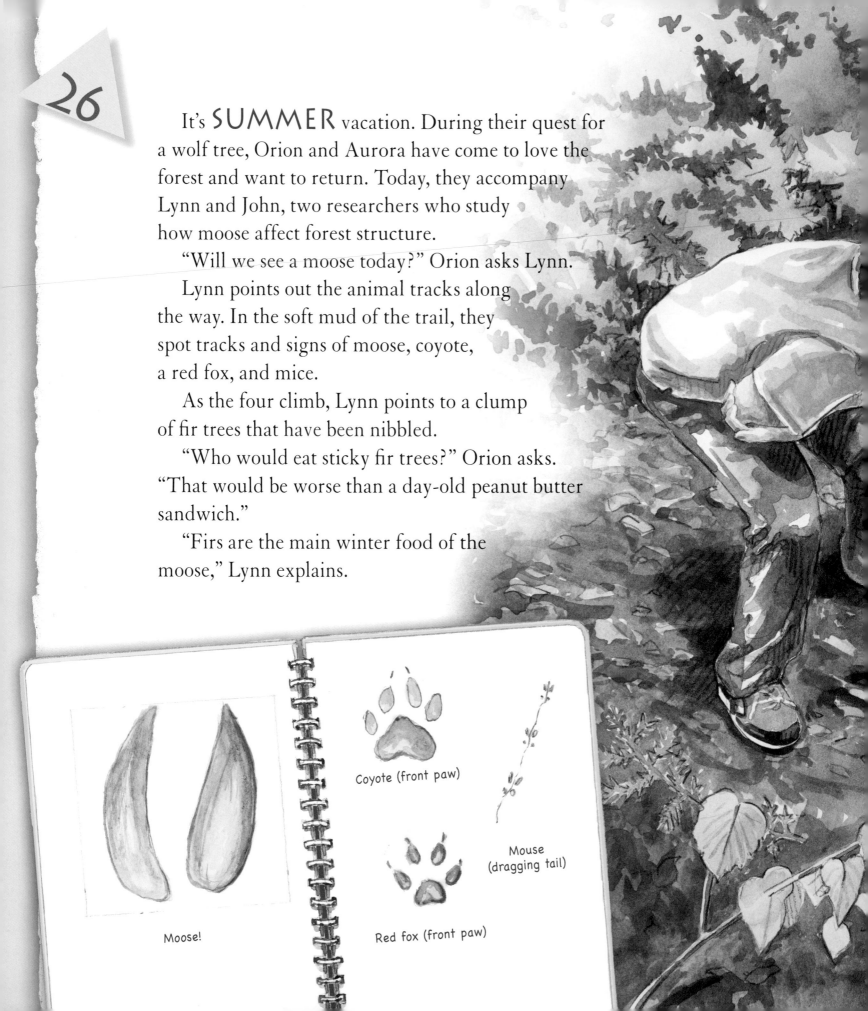

Moose!

Coyote (front paw)

Red fox (front paw)

Mouse (dragging tail)

The group climbs higher, crossing through the forest on the mountain slope. They all sit on a large log for lunch.

"Hey, that tree is HUGE!" Aurora exclaims. "How old do you think it is?" she asks.

John kneels down and twists a tree corer into the base of the spruce. He removes a core sample about nine inches long. Together, they count the **growth rings**, one ring for each year of growth.

"This tree may be over four hundred years old," John says.

From the sizable log where they had lunch to the many large trees they passed on the mountainside to this mighty red spruce, Orion and Aurora realize they are surrounded by a hillside of ancient trees.

"We've found a whole wolf pack!" Aurora exclaims.

"Yes, this is a fantastic find!" confirms John. "We call this type of forest **old growth**. You'll have to let the rangers know. This type of forest often needs special protection."

"Trying to find a wolf tree led us to so many amazing things," Orion tells the ranger.

"Yeah, we found a whole 'wolf pack' forest!" explains Aurora.

The ranger looks confused. "Wolf pack forest?" he asks.

"Oh, well John did say to tell you it was **old growth**," clarifies Orion.

"Great news! Where?" asks the ranger.

They all run over to the map. While they show the ranger the spot on Mount Kineo, he tells them they have become Junior Forest Rangers. He brings out special patches for them both. "This badge will let others know that you have a lot to share about the forest." He smiles.

"Congratulations on finding a wolf tree *and* locating a whole wolf pack forest!"

FROM ORION'S NOTEBOOK

Watershed: A piece of the landscape, roughly in a triangular shape, where all the precipitation eventually flows to a common drainage point.

Gage station: A place with instruments to measure the amount of precipitation (rain, snow, hail) and air temperature. At Hubbard Brook, there are twenty-four gage stations.

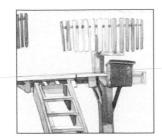

Old growth forest: A forest with no large disturbance for at least two hundred years. In these forests, there is a mixture of trees of all ages and stages, including many exceptionally old trees. These forests have become rare and deserve protection.

Weir: A permanent concrete structure that consists of a large pool area with a V-shaped metal notch at one end where the water flows out. The weir allows the volume of water passing to be calculated precisely.

Growth rings: The pattern of annual wood growth of a tree stem that when seen in cross section looks like a series of rings. The number of rings shows the age of the tree. The width of each ring shows how fast the tree grew in a particular year.

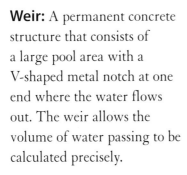

Succession: The steps of plant arrival and growth after a large disturbance, such as clear-cutting or a hurricane, which lead to different species of plants and animals being present in a place over time.

Production: In ecology, the amount of living material produced. Primary production is the new material made by plants, such as leaves, twigs, stems, roots, and seeds. Annual production is the amount of production within a given year.

Composition: The different types of objects that make up a sample. In the forest, composition typically refers to the different tree species present.

Mast years: Years when a plant or a group of plants of the same species produces much greater number of seeds (also called mast).

TIPS ON SPOTTING A WOLF TREE

☑ **Low branches:** Live canopy branches starting at about ⅓ to ½ the distance up the trunk.

☑ **Large trunk:** Trunk measures 50 cm or greater in diameter.

☑ **Signs of age:** Wear and tear on the tree; examples include broken canopy branches, broken lower branches, rotted areas, burls (bumps), and damage from lightning strikes.

☑ **Signs of wildlife use:** Marks or objects left by animals; examples include claw marks, scat (droppings), woodpecker holes, nest cavities, food remains, pieces of cones.

☑ **Surrounded by smaller trees:** Trees about ½ or less the diameter of the larger tree in question.